FATHERHOOD

Books by Derek Prince

Biography
Appointment in Jerusalem
Pages from My Life's Book

Guides to the Life of Faith
Baptism in the Holy Spirit
Blessing or Curse: You Can Choose!
Chords from David's Harp
Does Your Tongue Need Healing?
Extravagant Love
Faith to Live By
Fasting
Fatherhood
God Is a Matchmaker
God's Medicine Bottle
God's Plan for Your Money
God's Remedy for Rejection
How to Fast Successfully
If You Want God's Best
Life's Bitter Pool

Objective for Living: To Do God's Will
Prayers and Proclamations
Protection from Deception
Shaping History Through Prayer & Fasting
Spiritual Warfare
Thanksgiving, Praise and Worship
The Divine Exchange
The Grace of Yielding
The Holy Spirit in You
The Marriage Covenant
They Shall Expel Demons
Uproar in the Church

Systematic Bible Exposition
Foundations for Righteous Living
Christian Foundations Bible Correspondence Course
Self-Study Bible Course
The Destiny of Israel and the Church
The Last Word on the Middle East

DEREK PRINCE

FATHERHOOD

Derek Prince Ministries – UK
Harpenden, Hertfordshire

FATHERHOOD

Copyright © 1985 Derek Prince Ministries – International

Published by Derek Prince Ministries – UK 1999

ISBN 1 901144 08 9

This book is an edited transcript of *Fatherhood* from the *Today With
Derek Prince* daily radio programme.

Cover by Ronna Fu

Printed in the United Kingdom by
Stanley L Hunt, Rushden, Northants

Derek Prince Ministries
http://www.derekprince.com

CONTENTS

INTRODUCTION

One of the great themes of biblical revelation is fatherhood. Strangely enough, it is a theme that has been somewhat neglected in many Christian circles.

Personally, fatherhood is a subject which I have not merely studied in the Bible, but have also faced in my own experience. My first wife, Lydia, and I raised a family of nine. Subsequently, my second wife, Ruth, added three more children to our total family. So altogether I stand in the relationship of father to exactly one dozen persons. Most of them are grown and now have families of their own.

1
THE FATHERHOOD
OF GOD

However, it is not with human fatherhood that I want to begin. I want to share, first of all, about the fatherhood of God which is the great fact behind the universe. There is a Father who is our God and who also is the fact behind all other facts. It is a Father who created the universe, as a father, and who has left the imprint of His fatherhood on every aspect of the entire universe.

In Ephesians 3:14-15, Paul prays one of his great and wonderful prayers:

> For this cause I bow my knees unto the Father of our Lord Jesus Christ, [from] whom the whole family in heaven and earth [or every family in heaven and earth derives its] name.

> (KJV)

The word that is there translated "family" is the Greek word *patria*. And that word is derived directly from the Greek word for father, so the most literal, straightforward translation would be "fatherhood." In this connection, I would like to give you also J. B. Phillips translation of those verses which brings out this fact of the connection between father and family or fatherhood. Phillips translates it this way:

> When I think of the greatness of this great plan I fall on my knees before the Father (from whom all fatherhood, earthly or heavenly, derives its name). . . .
>
> (JBP)

That is a remarkable fact! All fatherhood in the universe ultimately goes back to the fatherhood of God; and that fatherhood did not begin on earth, it began in heaven. Fatherhood is eternal with God. It did not begin with time, it did not begin with human history, it began in eternity.

Eternally, God is the Father of our Lord Jesus Christ and He is so described in many parts of the Bible. In his gospel John says, "In the beginning . . . the Word was with God." That was before creation ever took place. The divine Word, the eternal Son of God, was with the Father. The Scripture says He was in the bosom of the Father. That intimate, personal relationship between God and the Son existed before creation ever began. This is an absolutely distinctive feature of Christian revelation. It makes Christianity unlike any other religious faith that I have ever encountered in the world. It reveals something unique and particular about the nature of God. In God, eternally, there is fatherhood. There is a relationship.

When Jesus came to earth, His ultimate purpose was to bring to the Father those who would turn to Him. This is stated in many places. 1 Peter 3:18 says:

> For Christ also died for sins once for all, the just for the unjust, in order that He might bring us to God. . . .
>
> (NAS)

Why did Jesus die? That He might bring us to God. Jesus was not the end, He was the way. He said that Himself, emphatically, in John 14:6:

> Jesus said . . . "I am the way, and the truth, and the life; no one comes to the Father, but through Me."

Jesus is the way, but the Father is the destination. I think many times in our Christian faith we really miss the purpose of God. We talk a great deal about the Lord Jesus Christ as our Saviour, our Intercessor, our Mediator, and so on. All of that is wonderful, but it stops short of God's purpose. God's purpose is not merely that we should come to the Son, but that through the Son we should come to the Father.

There is something beautiful about the language of Jesus in the prayer He prayed in John 17. This prayer opens with the word "Father" and it occurs six more times in the prayer. Jesus speaks about having made known the name of God to His disciples.

"I have manifested Thy name to the men
whom Thou gavest Me out of the world. . . ."

(verse 6, NAS)

Later He says:

"Holy Father, keep them in Thy name, the
name which Thou hast given Me. . . ."

(verse 11, NAS)

And right at the end of His prayer, He says again:

". . . I have made Thy name known to them,
and will make it known; that the love
wherewith Thou didst love Me may be in
them, and I in them."

(verse 26, NAS)

What name was it that Jesus came especially to make known to His disciples? It was not the sacred name Jehovah. The Jewish people had known that name for fifteen centuries. What was the new and special revelation, the great purpose, the name that Jesus wanted the disciples to know? The name is "Father." That is the ultimate name of God. That describes the nature of God in His eternal character more perfectly than any other word that exists in human language.

The ultimate revelation of God, therefore, in the New Testament, is the revelation of God as Father. And the ultimate purpose of the New Testament, the reason why Jesus Himself came, is to bring us to God. If we stop short of this revelation of God, we have stopped short of the full and final outworking of redemption's purpose.

When we come into the fullness of this revelation of God and into that direct relationship with God as Father, it supplies certain things which are conspicuously lacking in the emotional experience of perhaps the majority of the people in our culture. The three things which come out of this revelation and this relationship are: identity, self-worth, and security.

Identity

Identity is a real problem for modern man. An interesting commentary on this need was the success of the book and TV serial, *Roots*. The essence of that story was a man looking for the place or roots from which he came. All humanity is busy with the same search. Men and women want to know from where they came, who is behind them, how it started and who they are. Scripture and psychology agree that a person really does not answer the question, "Who am I?" until he or she knows who his or her father is.

Today, human relationships between parents and children have been so greatly broken down that it has produced an identity crisis. Christianity's answer to that identity crisis is to bring men and women into a direct, personal relationship with God the Father through Jesus Christ the Son. People who truly know God as Father no longer have an identity problem. They know who they are – they are children of God. Their Father created the universe, their Father loves them, and their Father cares for them.

Self-worth

That brings us to the second need that is supplied by this revelation of God the Father – the need of *self-worth.* I cannot count how many people I have dealt with in my ministry whose greatest problem was not sufficiently appreciating themselves. They had too low a picture of themselves which caused them many spiritual and emotional agonies. In 1 John 3:1, it says:

> See how great a love the Father has bestowed upon us, that we should be called children of God; and such we are.
>
> (NAS)

Once we really comprehend that we are the children of God, that God loves us intimately and personally, that He is interested in us, He is never too busy for us and He desires a direct and personal relationship with us, that gives us self-worth. I have seen this happen again and again in the lives of people.

Once I was in a meeting and I literally ran into a lady. We were going in opposite directions at considerable speed. She picked herself up and said, "Mr. Prince, I've been praying that if God wanted you to speak to me, we'd meet."

"Well," I said, "we've met. But I can only give you about two minutes. I'm very busy." She began to tell me what her problem was and after a while I interrupted her. I said, "I'm sorry, but I've only got one minute left . . . but I think I know your problem. Will you follow me in this prayer?" And I led her in a prayer in which she just thanked God because He was her Father and she was His child, that He loved her, that He cared for her, that she was special and that she belonged to the best family in the universe. I said, "Good-bye. I have to go," and left.

About a month later, I got a letter from that lady in which she said, "I just want to tell you that being together with you and praying that prayer has completely changed my attitude toward life. For the first time, I really have a sense of my own worth."

Security

The third great provision of God through the revelation of Father is *security*. Behind the universe is not just some scientific force or some "big bang," but a Father who loves us.

A friend of mine was once feeling lonely and sad late one night in the deserted, windy streets of a city. He just did not quite know if he was going to make it through. As he stood there on the street corner, he just began to say, over and over again, "Father . . . Father . . . Father . . . Father. . . ." As he did that, security came to him. He knew that even though things were cold and bleak around about him, he was a child of God in the universe that God had created for His children.

2
HUMAN
FATHERHOOD

Since the eternal character and nature of God is that of Father, it follows that every father, in a certain sense, represents God. In a certain sense, we may say that a father, a good father, is the most God-like thing a man can become. It is a man's highest achievement.

I remember a time when I was continually travelling from meeting to meeting and conference to conference, preaching to large crowds and having a good response from the people. But then I heard a man make this statement: "The expert is the man away from home with a briefcase." It went to my heart like an arrow. I thought to myself, "That really describes me. I'm a man away from home with a briefcase. Everybody regards me as an expert, but in actual fact, what's happening in my home?"

God challenged me, in an altogether new way, that I had to succeed, first and foremost, as a husband and as a father before I could succeed in any other capacity. To succeed in other capacities but fail as a father would be, in God's sight, to fail.

I believe this is true of many men in our culture today. They can succeed in many capacities: on the golf course, as the bank president, as an author, as an actor, maybe even as a Christian minister, and yet fail in their home. And I want to suggest to you that to fail in your home as a father is to fail, and no other success can make up for that failure.

In 1 Corinthians 11:3 Paul speaks about a relationship between God and the home. He says:

> But I want you to understand that Christ is the head of every man [or husband], and the man is the head of a woman, and God [the Father] is the head of Christ.

So, Christ is the head of the husband and the husband, in turn, is the head of his wife and his family. In a certain sense, therefore, the man (husband and father) represents Christ to his family. He has the same relationship to his family that Christ has to him.

There are three main ministries of Christ which are eternally associated with the Lord Jesus Christ: that of priest, that of prophet and that of king. Let me explain briefly what is involved in each ministry.

As a priest the father represents his family to God.
As a prophet he represents God to his family.
As a king he governs his family on behalf of God.

3
THE FATHER AS
A PRIEST

The father is the priest of his home, representing his family to God in intercession and prayer. A father's success in the other two ministries as prophet and king are very closely tied with his success as an intercessor and as a priest. If he succeeds as the intercessor, he will probably also succeed as the prophet and as the king. But if he does not understand the practice of the ministry of intercession for his family, then it will be very difficult for him to be either prophet or king in his family.

There are some very beautiful examples in the Bible of fathers who practised this ministry of intercession. At the opening of the book of Job we read that Job was a perfect and an upright man before God. He had seven sons and three daughters, and on one day of each week his family met in the house of one of his sons for feasting and fellowship. At the end of every week, Job rose up early and offered sacrifices on behalf of all of his sons, saying in his

heart that maybe they had failed and were not right with
God. So he would offer a sacrifice on their behalf.

The offering of those sacrifices of Job, in Old Testament
terminology, corresponds to the ministry of intercessory
prayer on behalf of our children under the new covenant in
Jesus Christ. Every father is called to be an intercessor for
his children.

Then we move on into the history of the nation of Israel
and find them enslaved in Egypt under darkness and
oppression. God made provision for their deliverance
through the sacrifice of the Passover lamb. The ultimate
point of separation between Israel and Egypt was the
Passover, which made provision for the deliverance of
every Israelite family. The destroying angel came into every
Egyptian home and slew the firstborn. But because of the
blood of the Passover lamb, the destroying angel was not
allowed to visit or destroy in any Israelite household. How
was that blood applied? Who applied it? Exodus 12:3:

> Speak ye unto all the congregation of
> Israel, saying, In the tenth day of this
> month they shall take to them every man a
> lamb, according to the house of their
> fathers, a lamb for an house. . . .
>
> (KJV)

Who was responsible to select the lamb? The father of
every family. Who was responsible to slay the lamb? The
father. Who was responsible to sprinkle its blood with
hyssop on the doorpost of his home? The father. In other
words, the father had the God-appointed ministry of priest
on behalf of his family. It was his responsibility to see that

God's provision of salvation was made effective in his particular home. As far as I understand the revelation of Scripture, no one else could do the father's job for him. If he fulfilled his function as priest and sprinkled the blood, his family would be safe. If he failed, there was no one else who could take his place and provide protection for his family.

I believe God has caused that revelation to come to us because it is still applicable today. There is something in the spiritual realm that a father can do for his house that he cannot delegate to anybody else. He can serve with a priestly ministry for his home which God will acknowledge, but God is not obliged to acknowledge that ministry in any other person but the father. It is the father's responsibility to provide divine protection for his home.

In the New Testament I would like to point out a remarkable fact about the ministry of Jesus. It is a fact that I have learned through personal experience. People have come to me to request prayer for a child and I have learned to ask, "Are you this child's parent? Are you the father or mother?" Sometimes the answer would be, "No. We're just neighbours; the parents didn't want to come." God showed me very definitely I had no scriptural basis for praying for a child like that. If you will study the ministry of Jesus, you will find that He never ministered to a child except on the basis of the faith of one or both parents. He always required a parent to exercise faith for a child.

This is very conspicuous in the story of the epileptic boy recorded in Mark 9. Jesus came down from the Mount of Transfiguration and He was confronted by a scene where His disciples had failed to cast out an epileptic spirit from a boy. Jesus began to talk to the father and He asked the father how long the boy had suffered. The father replied, "Since he was a child." Then he went on to say:

> And ofttimes it hath cast him into the fire, and into the waters, to destroy him: but if thou canst do any thing, have compassion on us, and help us. Jesus said unto him, If thou canst believe, all things are possible to him that believeth.
>
> (Mark 9:22-23, KJV)

One day I was gripped by the realisation that Jesus held the father responsible to believe for his son. The son, because of his condition, obviously could not exercise much faith for himself, but, in any case, Jesus did not ask the son to exercise faith. He required the father to exercise faith on behalf of his son. I believe it is the responsibility of parents to exercise faith in intercessory prayer on behalf of their children and bring them to God through Jesus Christ. You can search the Scriptures for yourself and you will find Jesus never ministered to a child unless there was at least one parent exercising faith on behalf of that child. He would not go contrary to such a deeply entrenched principle of God.

Finally, look at Acts 16:31 where we find the story of the Philippian jailer. Paul and Silas had been imprisoned, then God intervened with an earthquake, the prison doors were opened and the people's chains were loosed. The jailer sprang in and he said, "Sirs, what must I do to be saved?" Verse 31 says:

> . . . Believe on the Lord Jesus Christ, and

thou shalt be saved, and thy house[hold].

(KJV)

You will notice that the jailer, as the father of his house, was afforded the God-given privilege of exercising faith for the salvation of his whole house. Too many times, alas, in quoting that Scripture, we tend to leave out those last three words, ". . . and thy house[hold]."

4
THE FATHER AS PROPHET

A father's second main responsibility is prophet for his family; that is, to represent God to his family.

The first thing we need to see is that inevitably a father does represent God to his family. He may intend to do it, he may do it well or he may do it badly but, almost inevitably, he does it. Psychiatrists, sociologists and those in ministry would almost all agree that a child normally forms its first impression of God from its father. I believe this was intended by God. One of the most solemn responsibilities that God can give any human being is to represent Himself to others.

The kind of father a person had has a lot to do with that person's initial response and reaction to God. If a person had a father who was kind, outgoing, warm-hearted and easy to communicate with, that person will normally find it easy to think of and to approach God in those terms. But if a person had a father who was unkind, critical and always

making unreasonable and excessive demands, that person is
liable to think of God in the same way. They will see God
as always making demands which humanity can never live
up to: unrealistic, legalistic and harsh. Sometimes it
happens that a child has a father who is actually cruel and
vicious. Very frequently such a child unconsciously
transfers those attributes from the natural human father to
God. Consequently, they have a negative attitude to God
which is not based on any reason except the behaviour of
the father.

How can a father represent God to his family – to be the
prophet for good and not for evil? In Ephesians 6:4, Paul is
writing to fathers as he says:

> And, fathers, do not provoke your children
> to anger; but bring them up in the discipline
> and instruction of the Lord.
>
> (NAS)

Again, in Colossians 3:21:

> Fathers, do not exasperate your children,
> that they may not lose heart.
>
> (NAS)

The New Testament, just like the Old Testament, places
the responsibility for the spiritual education and instruction
of the children fairly and squarely upon the shoulders of the
father. Obviously, mothers have a great influence over
children and a lot to contribute to their spiritual
development, but, primarily, it is the father who is
responsible for providing spiritual instruction for his

children. If a father does not do it, there is no one else who can exactly take over that responsibility.

The majority of fathers, if they are aware that they have any responsibility for the instruction of their children, are quite content to transfer it to the Sunday school, to the church, to the pastor or to the youth leader. Very often such a parent, if his child is in some kind of church or youth group and goes astray, will blame the church or the youth group. The father can never divest himself as the primary responsibility for raising his children in the discipline and instruction of the Lord. It is one of his sacred responsibilities which is not transferable.

Paul indicates that in doing this a father must guard against two opposite dangers. The first danger is *rebelliousness* in the child. The father guards against rebellion by maintaining firm discipline – not allowing children to become wayward or irresponsible, not allowing them to answer back and expecting them to do what they are told promptly, quietly, obediently. It is much easier to give instruction to children who are brought up that way.

However, a father must also guard against the opposite extreme which is *discouragement*. If a father is unduly severe, critical and demanding, the result may be that the child will become discouraged and take the attitude, "Well, it's no good. Nothing I do ever pleases my father, so I might as well not bother to try." The warning that Paul gives is: "Don't provoke them. Don't exasperate them."

I have dealt with many people who had severe emotional problems and had come to me for help. I cannot tell you how many times I have discovered that their negative attitude – lack of self-worth, feeling of failure, frustration – goes back to a time in that person's life when, as a child, they experienced negative treatment, such as criticism, being put down or scolded unfairly in front of others. That treatment left a mark or wound in the soul of that child which has not healed for maybe twenty or thirty years. Fathers must be careful to maintain discipline on the one hand but, on the other hand, not to discourage or exasperate their children by unfair or excessive demands.

In order to meet his responsibilities to his family, a father must always keep in mind the need for regular, ongoing communication with his children. If he does not maintain that kind of communication, then he cannot fulfil his responsibilities. The communication between a father and his child is usually most effective in a non-religious setting. If children associate the instruction their father gives them with something stiff, formal and religious, they tend, in the end, to resent both the religion and the instruction. I can think of a good many cases of people whose problems went back to that kind of situation.

It is essential in communicating with children to not merely talk to them but to let them talk to you. Most people who deal with wayward or delinquent children would agree that they nearly always have one common complaint: "Our parents never listen to us." So you must cultivate the practice of listening. Let your child talk, let him or her express themselves, let them come out with their problem and do not try to do it in too religious an atmosphere.

This principle is stated in the law where Moses gave the Israelites very clear and practical instructions on how to bring up their children. Deuteronomy 11:18-21:

> Therefore shall ye lay up these my words in
> your heart and in your soul. . . . And ye

shall teach them [to] your children,
speaking of them when thou sittest in thine
house, and when thou walkest by the way,
when thou liest down, and when thou risest
up. And thou shalt write them on the door
posts of thine house, and upon thy gates:
That your days may be multiplied, and the
days of your children, in the land which the
LORD sware unto your fathers to give
them, as the days of heaven upon the earth.
(KJV)

I was impressed when I discovered that the phrase ". . .
heaven on earth" came from the Bible. Furthermore, it was
a description of what God expected the families of His
people to be like. I looked around at our modern civilisation
and I said to myself, "How many families in this nation
today could be described as 'heaven on earth'?" I would
say, frankly, it is a very small proportion.

One main reason for this is that fathers have failed to do
what Moses said they should do. Moses said, in effect,
"Teach the Word of God, the truths of your faith, to your
children. Speak about them when you sit down, when you
rise up, when you walk by the way." In other words, let the
Word of God be a central theme of your whole family life.
Do not simply reserve the teaching of Scripture to the
church, Sunday school or youth group. Let God's Word
have a natural place in your daily life and communication
with your family. Let it be something natural and something
practical. Let the children see how it works out in real-life
situations.

I would like to quote the testimony of the late Dr. V.

Raymond Edman, one-time president of Wheaton College, who said: "Looking back on the way I brought up my children, if I had to do it over, I'd spend more time with them in simple, non-religious activities." To that I would have to say, "Amen." If I could live some of the time I have spent with my children again, that is what I would do. Dr. Edman found that the things the grown children remembered most were the informal times of just being together.

Real communication with a child is not achieved in five minutes. Often the most important things are said with a child in a casual or off-hand way at a time when you would least expect it. For instance, on a fishing trip, gardening, mowing the lawn, cleaning out the garage or finding out why the car will not run. It is situations like these which lend themselves to real communication between parents and children. It is in those kinds of situations that a father should be able to transmit to his child the deep principles of the Word of God. Just having "a family altar" by itself will not necessarily do it. A lot depends on how the rest of the time is spent in the family.

5
THE FATHER AS KING

The function of a king, of course, is to rule or to govern and is the third ministry of the father in his home.

In modern America, the word "king" is not always too acceptable, although it is a word that is used throughout the Bible. If you do not like the word king, we can substitute the word "governor." In any case, the function of the father is to rule or govern his household on behalf of God.

If we turn to 1 Timothy, Paul discusses the qualifications for a man who wants to hold the position of an elder, overseer, or a bishop. Various different words are used, but the point is, it is the description of a man who is to lead or to govern God's people. The most important of all the qualifications for that office is the condition of the man's home. How does that man function in his home? This is what Paul says in 1 Timothy 3:4-5:

[Such a man] must have proper authority in

his own household, and be able to control
and command the respect of his children.
(For if a man cannot rule in his own house
how can he look after the Church of God?)

(JBP)

A man is expected to rule in his own house. He is
expected to exercise authority and to have his children
respectful, obedient and under his control. If a man cannot
achieve that at home, Paul indicates he has no hope of
succeeding as a ruler, governor or leader in God's church.

The word that is used there for "to rule" literally, in
Greek, means "to stand out in front" or "to stand at the head
of." It contains various related ideas. I would just like to
give you a few different ways you could understand it: to
rule, to lead, to stand at the head, to protect, to control.
Essentially, it means that the father is the head of his home,
he is out in front, he sets an example and he stands between
his family and all the dangers and pressures of life. It means
that he is a man. He has what it takes. He has what modern
speech calls "guts." It takes "guts" to be a man and to be a
father.

Paul then goes on to say successful leadership at home is
essential for leadership in the church. There is strong reason
for this: The home is really the church in miniature, in
microcosm or in embryo.

In the church there are three main elements: the pastor or
the shepherd; the deacon or the helper; and the congregation
or the flock. Those correspond to the three main elements in
the home. In the home, the father has the responsibilities of
the pastor or shepherd. The wife, according to Scripture, is
the helper, created to help her husband like the deacon. The

children are the congregation or the flock. God has built into the family all the basics that make up a proper New Testament church. God says, in effect, to the father of the family, "You make it succeed in your little church, the one I've committed to you in your own home, and then you'll qualify for promotion in the church of God."

Let me say this also, as a matter of observation and experience: You can build a large congregation of people who attend a church, but in the last resort, a congregation is no stronger than the families that make it up. If the families are not in order, the church cannot be in order.

As a picture of a father who accepted and fulfilled his responsibility to rule, govern, or be king of his home, I want to turn now to Abraham. There is a very significant passage in Genesis 18 where the Lord is speaking about Abraham. He reveals why He chose Abraham to be the head of the new nation that was ultimately to bring redemption to all humanity.

I do not know whether you have ever wondered why God chose Abraham. Doubtless there were hundreds of thousands of contemporaries of Abraham all over the earth's surface. Out of all of those hundreds of thousands, God chose one man. Is it an unrevealed mystery why God chose Abraham? No, it is not. Because God Himself tells us just why He chose that one man, Abraham, to be the head of this new race on which the salvation of all other races was going to depend. Genesis 18:17-19:

> And the LORD said, Shall I hide from
> Abraham that thing which I do; Seeing that
> Abraham shall surely become a great and
> mighty nation, and all the nations of the

> earth shall be blessed in him? For I know
> him, that he will command his children and
> his household after him, and they shall keep
> the way of the Lord, to do justice and
> judgement; that the Lord may bring upon
> Abraham that which he hath spoken of him.
>   (KJV)

First, look at the meaning of Abraham's name. Originally, his name was Abram, which means "exalted father." Then, when God made His covenant, blessed him and promised him a great number of descendants, God changed his name to Abraham, which means "father of a multitude." But you will see in both forms that the first fact about his name is that he is a father. That is tremendously significant. God chose Abraham as a father.

Second, fatherhood, when its duties are carried out, builds a mighty nation. God said of Abraham, ". . . [he] shall surely become a great and mighty nation." Why? Because he could be relied upon to fulfil his obligations as a father.

Third, why did God choose Abraham? He states it Himself. He says, "I know him, that he will command his children and his household after him, and they shall keep the way of the Lord, to do justice and judgement; that the Lord may bring upon Abraham that which he hath spoken of him." What did God see in Abraham that made Him choose him? He saw that he would command his children and his household after him to keep the way of the Lord. He could rely on Abraham to fulfil his duties as a governor of his family.

That word "command" is a strong word. It is almost a military word. There may be some mothers or wives who would ask, "Are you speaking about being a dictator?" No, but I am speaking about a man who is a man – a man who knows his position and responsibility. There are some situations in which a man under God is responsible to command his household. He is responsible to say, "In order to please God and have His blessing, this is the way we're going to do it in our home. We're *not* going to do this, but we *are* going to do that." A father has a right to determine some of the basic rules of the household: what time they will eat together, the time that younger children must be in, the kind of entertainments that are permitted, the amount of time that they spend in front of television and the kind of programmes they watch. A father has not merely the privilege, he has the duty of commanding his family in these respects. God said, "I'll bring upon Abraham that which I've promised because I can trust him to do that for Me."

Fourth, all through the rest of the Scripture, Abraham is set forth as a pattern for all subsequent believers. In fact, the New Testament says that we are the children of Abraham by faith and that we are to walk in the steps of the faith of our father, Abraham. Walking in the steps of Abraham's faith means that we behave in our homes as Abraham behaved in his home.

In closing this section, let me draw a contrast. There was another man who went a long way with Abraham, knew a lot of what Abraham knew and saw a lot of what God did for Abraham. His name was Lot. But the time came for Abraham and Lot to separate because their flocks and herds were too numerous for them to stay together. Abraham, like the gentleman that he was, said to Lot, "You choose. Whichever way you go, I'll go the opposite." Lot chose to go toward Sodom, a place of extreme sinfulness. The next time we read about Lot, he and his family were inside Sodom and the judgement of God was about to come on the city. Lot tried desperately to get his sons-in-law and most of his family out and failed. As he escaped himself and looked back upon the smouldering ruins of Sodom, he must have realised that many of his family had been destroyed in that ruin and that he was responsible for taking them in.

Fathers, you may lead your children into Sodom, but you may not be able to lead them out again. What a fearful responsibility rested upon the shoulders of Lot as a father. He led his children into a place of sin and ultimate judgement and could not get them out again.

6
WHEN FATHERS FAIL

S uppose that a father fails? What happens to his family?
Or suppose that the fathers in a nation fail. What
happens to that nation? Because God knew that Abraham
would fulfil his duties as a father, God promised that he
would become a great and mighty nation. But what about a
nation whose fathers do not fulfil their duties?

In Deuteronomy 28 Moses lists two things: first, the
blessings that will come upon God's people if they obey
Him; secondly, the curses that will come upon them if they
disobey Him. The first fourteen verses contain the
blessings. The remaining verses of the chapter, verses 15
through 68, list the curses for the disobedience of not
walking in God's way and not keeping God's law.

Now there are many remarkable curses listed, but I want
to point out just one. In Deuteronomy 28:41, Moses says:

Thou shalt beget sons and daughters, but

>   thou shalt not enjoy them; for they shall go
>   into captivity.
>
> (KJV)

The language that Moses uses is in the masculine. In other words, it is addressed primarily to fathers. Also the word "beget" primarily refers to the father's part in procreating children. So this is addressed primarily, but not exclusively, to fathers. It says, "Thou shalt beget sons and daughters, but thou shalt not enjoy them." It came to me with a shock one day that not enjoying our children is a curse. I began to ask myself, "How many parents really enjoy their children today?"

I was reminded of a pastor, a friend of mine, who had a large family of children and I remember hearing him pray one day, "Lord, help us to remember that children are a blessing and not a burden." I did not feel somehow, that he was praying with very strong faith. I think that the majority of parents really do not enjoy their children. Why not? What is the reason? It is a curse for disobedience. God gave children as the greatest blessing He could give to men and women. When fathers and mothers, and especially fathers, do not walk in the way of the Lord, then that blessing is no longer a blessing. Moses warns the fathers of Israel that if they do not keep God's way and walk in it, then, "You will not enjoy your children, for they shall go into captivity."

In these last two decades, we have seen millions of children go into various kinds of satanic captivity – to drugs, illicit sex, the occult and various types of cults. That is captivity just a surely as if an invading alien army had come into the country and carried them off prisoners. Why did these millions of children go into captivity? The answer is given there in the Scriptures. Because their fathers failed in their responsibilities. The primary responsibility for that state of affairs in modern society rests at the door of fathers.

We hear a lot about juvenile delinquents. There are hardly any juvenile delinquents until there are first adult delinquents. It takes adult delinquents to bring forth juvenile delinquents.

I pointed out earlier that one of the father's responsibilities to his family was that of a priest. In Malachi 2:7, the Lord states what is required of a priest:

> For the priest's lips should keep knowledge, and they should seek the law at his mouth: for he is the messenger of the LORD of hosts.
>
> (KJV)

It is the responsibility of the priest to know the law of the Lord and to interpret it to the Lord's people. So the priest is the messenger, or perhaps a better word would be "representative," of the Lord to His people. This applies, as we have already seen, to the father as priest. His lips should keep knowledge. His children and his family should seek the Lord God at his mouth. He should be God's representative to them.

What happens if priests fail in this function? If we turn to Hosea 4:6, God declares what He will do to a family, to a nation or to a civilisation when its priests fail:

> My people are destroyed for lack of

> knowledge [not scientific knowledge, but
> the knowledge of the way and the word of
> the LORD]: because thou hast rejected
> knowledge, I will also reject thee, that thou
> shalt be no priest to me: seeing thou hast
> forgotten the law of thy God, I will also
> forget thy children.
>
> (KJV)

That is a very powerful word to fathers. God says, in effect, "I expected you to be the priest of your family. But because you have rejected the knowledge that your family needs, I am going to reject you. I will no longer accept you as priest. And when your priestly ministry on behalf of your children is no longer accepted by Me," God says, "then I will also forget your children."

That is frightening! To think that God would say to us, as parents, "You've so failed in your responsibility that I'm going to forget your children. I am just going to be toward them as if they were not there. I am going to write them off. They are of no more consequence or significance before Me." I would say that this nation of ours, this civilisation of ours, is filled with God-forgotten children. Why? Because their fathers did not keep the law of the Lord.

Let me say it this way: The father who rejects the knowledge of God's law loses his right to be a priest to his family. When the father's priestly ministry is no longer available, God says, "I will forget your children." That is a very, very solemn thought.

In closing, I want to turn to the last two verses of the Old Testament. I do not know whether you have ever reflected on the fact that the last word of the Old Testament in the

generally used translation is the word "curse." It is a very
solemn thought that if God had no more to say to man after
the Old Testament, His last word to humanity would have
been a curse. Thank God for the New Testament which
shows the way out of the curse.

This is what God says in these last two verses of the book
of Malachi, Malachi 4:5-6:

> Behold, I will send you Elijah the prophet
> before the coming of the great and dreadful
> day of the LORD. And he shall turn the heart
> of the fathers to the children, and the heart
> of the children to their fathers, lest I come
> and smite the earth with a curse.
>
> (KJV)

I am impressed by the tremendous insight of prophetic
revelation, in that, well over two thousand years ago,
Malachi was able to foresee the greatest and most urgent
social problem of our day. What is that problem? It is
divided, strife-torn homes. Fathers and children out of
relationship. The children rebellious, the fathers negligent.
And the prophet warns us if this state of affairs does not
change, it is going to bring a curse on that unit; whether it
be a family, or a nation or a civilisation. God's Word faces
us with just two alternatives in our current situation today:
we may either restore family relationships and survive; or
we may allow family relationships to deteriorate and go the
way they have been going the last decades. If we do the
latter, we will perish under God's curse. Those are the
alternatives.

In a very significant sense, the destiny will be settled by

the fathers. It is the fathers whom God holds responsible. Because God could trust Abraham to be the kind of father that He wanted, He said, "He'll become a great and mighty nation." But the contrary is also true. Where fathers fail and do not fulfil their responsibilities, a nation can no longer remain great. I believe that is the very crisis that confronts our nation today. Are the fathers going to return to God and face their responsibilities to their families in the sight of God? Or is the present moral and social breakdown, which originated in the family and is destroying the family, going to continue and come to its ultimate consequence, which is a curse?

It will be the decision of the fathers that determines the destiny of the nation. God requires the fathers to turn to the children. Then He promises the children will return to their fathers.

ABOUT THE AUTHOR

Derek Prince was born in India, of British parents. He was educated as a scholar of Greek and Latin at two of Britain's most famous educational institutions – Eton College and Cambridge University. From 1940 to 1949 he held a Fellowship in Ancient and Modern Philosophy at King's College, Cambridge. He also studied Hebrew and Aramaic, at both Cambridge University and the Hebrew University in Jerusalem. In addition he speaks a number of other modern languages.

In the early years of World War II, while serving as a hospital attendant with the British Army, Derek Prince experienced a life-changing encounter with Jesus Christ, concerning which he writes:

> Out of this encounter, I formed two conclusions that I have never since had reason to change: first, that Jesus Christ is

alive; second, that the Bible is a true,
relevant, up-to-date book. These two
conclusions radically and permanently
altered the whole course of my life.

At the end of World War II, he remained where the
British Army had placed him – in Jerusalem. Through his
marriage to his first wife, Lydia, he became father to the
eight adopted girls in Lydia's children's home there.
Together the family saw the rebirth of the State of Israel in
1948. While serving as educators in Kenya, Derek and
Lydia adopted their ninth child, an African baby girl. Lydia
died in 1975. In 1978 he married Ruth Baker. For 20 years
they travelled the world together imparting God's revealed
truth and sharing his prophetic insight into world events in
the light of scripture. Ruth passed away in December 1998.

Derek Prince's non-denominational, non-sectarian
approach has opened doors for his teaching to people from
many different racial and religious backgrounds, and he is
internationally recognised as one of the leading Bible
expositors of our time. His daily radio broadcast, "Today
with Derek Prince," reaches more than half the world in
thirteen languages, including Chinese, Russian, Arabic and
Spanish.

Some of Derek Prince's more than forty books have been
translated into over sixty different languages. Since 1989
there has been special focus on Eastern Europe and the
C.I.S. (former U.S.S.R.), with over one million copies of his
books circulating in the languages of those nations. His
Video Bible School is the foundation for dozens of new
Bible schools in this previously unreached part of the world.

Through their Global Outreach Programme, Derek

Prince Ministries has given away hundreds of thousands of books and audio cassettes to pastors and leaders in more than 120 nations – to those who either had no access to teaching materials or who had no funds with which to buy them.

Now past the age of eighty, Derek continues to travel widely, ministering as the Lord directs.

The international base of Derek Prince Ministries is located in Charlotte, North Carolina, with offices in Australia, Canada, France, Germany, Netherlands, New Zealand, Singapore, South Africa and the United Kingdom. There are also distributors in many other nations.

DEREK PRINCE MINISTRIES
OFFICES WORLDWIDE

AUSTRALIA
DPM – Australia
1st Floor, 134 Pendle Way
Pendle Hill
New South Wales 2145
Australia
Tel: + 612 9688 4488
Fax: + 612 9688 4848
E-mail: enquiries@au.derekprince.com

CANADA
DPM – Canada
PO Box 8354
Halifax N.S.
B3K 5M1 Canada
Tel/Fax: + 1 902 443 9577
E-mail: enquiries@ca.derekprince.com

FRANCE
DPM – France
Route d'Oupia, BP 31
34210 Olonzac
France
Tel: + 33 468 913872
Fax: + 33 468 913863
E-mail: enquiries@fr.derekprince.com

GERMANY
DPM – Germany
Schwarzauer Str. 56
D-83308 Trostberg
Germany
Tel: + 49 8621 64146
Fax: + 49 8621 64147
E-mail: enquiries@de.derekprince.com

NETHERLANDS
DPM – Netherlands
PO Box 349
1960 AH Heemskerk
The Netherlands
Tel: + 31 251 255 044
Fax: + 31 251 247 798
E-mail: enquiries@nl.derekprince.com

SINGAPORE
Derek Prince Publications Pte Ltd
PO Box 2046
Robinson Road Post Office
Singapore 904046
Tel: + 65 392 1812
Fax: + 65 392 1823
E-mail: enquiries@sg.derekprince.com

SOUTH AFRICA
DPM – South Africa
PO Box 33367
Glenstantia 0010
Pretoria
South Africa
Tel: + 27 12 348 9537
Fax: + 27 12 348 9538
E-mail: enquiries@za.derekprince.com

UNITED KINGDOM
DPM – UK
PO Box 77
Harpenden
Hertfordshire AL5 1PJ
UK
Tel: 01582 466200
Fax: 01582 766777
E-mail: enquiries@uk.derekprince.com

SOUTH PACIFIC
DPM – South Pacific
224 Cashel Street
PO Box 2029
Christchurch 8015
New Zealand
Tel: + 64 3 366 4443
Fax: + 64 3 366 1569
E-mail: enquiries@nz.derekprince.com

USA
DPM – USA
PO Box 19501
Charlotte
NC 28219-9501
USA
Tel: + 1 704 357 3556
Fax: + 1 704 357 1413
E-mail: enquiries@us.derekprince.com